# Knitted Cats

## Joy Gammon

**Search Press**

Be they plain moggies or pampered thoroughbreds, all cats have great charm and character. I have tried to include a pet to suit all tastes and I hope you will enjoy making them as much as I did. Your finishing touches will give them their own highly individual personalities.

*Joy Gammon*

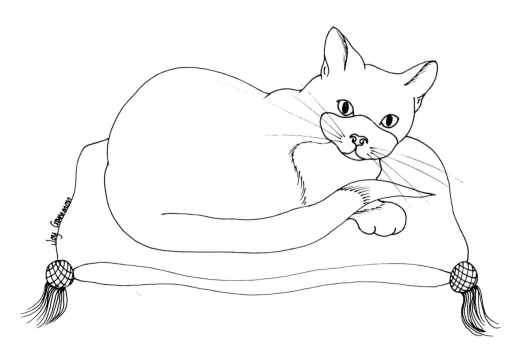

# Introduction

Cats are strange, magical creatures and humans have always been fascinated by them. I like to think that, whereas dogs consider they are human, cats know that they are not but believe themselves to be our infinite superiors! We worship them, admire them and are allowed to look after them. Yet in spite of their aloofness, or perhaps because of it, and certainly because of their beauty and charm, we welcome them warmly as members of our family.

Many people collect cats, not just the real thing but china cats, stone cats, cloth cats, toy cats, painted cats, jewel cats and books on cats. To this you can now add knitted cats. From this book you can make your own versions of the ideal pet but you won't have to ask someone to feed them when you go away on holiday, nor deal with the well-intentioned dead mice offerings every morning. Whether your preference runs to a macho moggie, or a sophisticated Siamese, these fluffy knitted felines make wonderful toys, cushions and companions.

# Tools and materials

**Needles**: exact knitting needle requirements are given in the instructions for each cat. Other requirements are stitch holders, row counters and blunt- ended sewing needles for seaming with wool (tapestry needles).

**Yarns**: see the individual patterns for exact requirements. The colours are your personal choice. You will need oddments of yarns for embroidering features and paws.

**Filling**: the cats are filled with washable man-made fibres. It is worth investing in this as home-made fillings, such as fabric oddments and cut-up stockings or tights, are often heavy and dark in colour and may show through the knitting.

**Extras**: safety eyes and noses for toys are available in various sizes and colours. All sorts of other extras may be added as the fancy takes you. The odd-eyed white kitten, for instance, has a pretty blue bow around her neck.

# Stitches and abbreviations

Most of the cats are knitted in stocking stitch (abbreviated to st st), made by knitting and purling alternate rows, see page 30 for basic know-how. The other side is known as reverse stocking stitch (rev st st). Other general abbreviations used in this book are as follows:

| | |
|---|---|
| alt | alternate(ly) |
| beg | begin(ning) |
| cont | continu(e)(ing) |
| dec | decreas(e)(ing) |
| DK | double knitting |
| foll | follow(ing) |
| gm | gram |
| inc | increas(e)(ing) |
| kg | kilogram |
| K | knit |
| K-wise | knit wise |
| M1 | make one by picking up the loop which lies between the needles and knit through the back of the loop to increase a stitch |
| P | purl |
| rem | remain(ing) |
| rep | repeat |
| st | stitch(es) |
| tog | together |
| tbl | through back of loop |

The numbers shown in parenthesis, ( ), refer to the larger size.

# Sizes and tensions

All the cats featured in this book are made from three basic patterns: the lying down cat, the curled up cat and the sitting cat. Each pattern has two sizes and further size variations are achieved by using thicker or thinner yarns and their appropriate needles.

The patterns are set out in stitch and row numbers so that the proportions will remain correct however much the yarns vary. You, of course, can use the patterns with any yarn you wish at a suitable tension to achieve the size and colour of cat you desire. If you wish to use the yarns as given in this book, approximate tensions are shown in the individual cat patterns.

# Knitting yarns quantities and conversions

Most yarns available in the UK are marketed by weight rather than by yardage. The density of dye used to obtain certain colours may result in more or less yarn in each ball, although the composition of yarn is exactly the same. The following conversions are provided as a guide:

25 gm – 0.9 oz
50 gm – 1.8 oz
100 gm – 3.6 oz

# Methods and techniques

**The three basic patterns**: the main patterns and general finishing instructions for the lying down cat, curled up cat and sitting cat, are shown at the beginning of each section. Each basic pattern is followed by details of how the individual cat is created, giving the pattern and yarn details required to achieve the final effect. Instructions in the basic patterns are clearly listed in alphabetical sequence so that when you make your chosen pattern variation you can easily refer back to the basic instructions: as an example, the grey short-haired cat, shown on page 21, is in the lying down position and all the step-by-step instructions are listed under the basic pattern for this model, (see page 18). Only specific details of tools and materials stitch and feature variations, are given in the individual pattern (see page 20).

**Making up and finishing:** this is vitally important and can make all the difference between success and, at the best, peculiar results, so to help you with the finishing process each basic pattern has its own making up instructions. Always match shapings and ease any fullness in to match before seaming. I usually use back stitch for straight seams, and oversew the finished filled pieces together as invisibly as possible. Tease filling out well and do not over fill because knitting stretches and will distort, causing the filling to show.

# Finishing touches

Remember to aim for caricature. Be as realistic as possible but with simplicity rather than fussiness. If possible, use a real cat as your model, or work from photographs or sketches. Believe what you see – cats' heads really are almost round and their surprisingly large ears do grow vertically from the sides of their heads.

**Eyes**: safety eyes are very realistic and successful and, of course, safe. Remember, though, to be quite sure of where you want to place them before attaching the washer at the back of the knitting, as they are virtually irremoveable. Most of the cats featured in this book have 'eye make-up' which creates an oval shape. Take a line of embroidery from the inner corner over to the outer corner of the eye. On many cats this line extends from the inner corner of the eye down to the outer edge of the nose and the nose itself is a darker colour (see Fig 1).

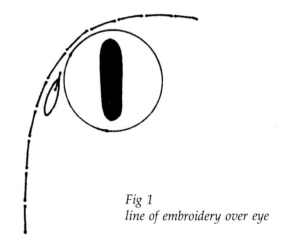

*Fig 1*
*line of embroidery over eye*

**Noses**: cats' noses are often pink, or of the same dark colour as their fur. I embroidered the characteristic petal-shape on to the cats' noses, (see Fig 2), and in some cases used a darker line of embroidery immediately below the main colour to enhance the nose shape. Safety noses are realistic and successful. I gave the grey short-haired cat a safety nose which shows up well on his dark colour.

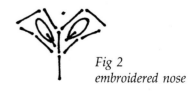

*Fig 2*
*embroidered nose*

**Muzzles**: cats' muzzles divide immediately below the nose and, with straight stitches, this line can be added then divided into the characteristic inverted 'Y' shape which then curves up at either side, (see Fig 3), or remains straight and short on grumpy-faced breeds, (see Fig 4).

*Fig 3*
*embroidered muzzle*

*Fig 4*
*embroidered muzzle for grumpy-faced breeds*

**Mouths**: if you use a dark or black yarn for your cat, an added mouth may not be necessary as the seam is an effective mouth mark. But on lighter yarns an embroidered mouth adds character.

**Whiskers**: no cat is complete without its whiskers. These are usually white, and I have used ordinary yarn, cut into suitable lengths and stitched firmly on to the face at one end. I had to cut the lengths of yarn fairly short or the whiskers drooped, which is not suitable for all breeds of cat, although to some it adds character and a certain charm.

**Ears**: these are very important for both character and expression. Apart from the Persian and long-haired breeds whose ears tend to be an inverted 'V' the longest edge of most cats' ears is vertical to the side of the head. These then curve at the base to support the shape.

**Watchpoint**:
If the cats are to be given to small children, remember safety and ensure that all materials used are washable, non-toxic and that all trimmings are very firmly attached. Mohair and angora yarn are unsuitable for very small children.

# Curled up cats

*From the basic pattern for the curled up cat, make the tabby, the two playful kittens, the tortoiseshell and white cat and the white Persian.*

## Basic pattern

### Body top and base (make two)

a) Cast on 20 (30)sts.

b) Inc one st at each end of every row until there are 32 (46) sts then inc one st at each end of every alt row until there are 40 (60) sts.

c) Work 14 (22) rows without shaping.

d) Dec one st at each end of next, then every alt row until 32 (46) sts remain.

e) Dec one st at each end of every row until 20 (30) sts remain.

f) Cast off.

### Head

g) Cast on 8 sts and work 1 row.

h) Next row – Inc one st in every st (16) sts.
Work 1 row.

i) Next row – (Inc one st in next st, work 2, inc one st in next st) 4 times. (24) sts.
Work 1 row.
Next row – (Inc one st in next st, work 4, inc one st in next st) 4 times. (32) sts.
Work 1 row.

j) Cont in this way, adding 8 sts on every alt row by working 2 more sts between increasings on each increasing row, until there are 48 (72) sts.

k) Work 13 (19) rows without shaping.

l) Next row – *Work 2 tog, work 8 (14), work 2 tog tbl, rep from * to end. 40 (64) sts.

Work 1 row.
Next row – *Work 2 tog, work 6 (12), work 2 tog tbl, rep from * to end. 32 (56) sts.
Work 1 row.

m) Cont in this way, losing 8 sts on every alt row, and, so working 2 sts less between decreasings on each decreasing row until there are 8 sts.
Run a thread through rem sts.

### Feet (make four)

n) Cast on 5 (7) sts and work 1 row.

o) Next row – Inc one st in every st. 10 (14) sts.
Rep the last 2 rows once more. 20 (28) sts.

p) Work 6 (8) rows without shaping.

q) *** Next row – *Work 2 tog, rep from * to end. 10 (14) sts.
Work 1 row.
Rep the last 2 rows once more.
Run a thread through rem 5 (7) sts.

### Tail

r) Cast on 20 (28) sts.

s) Work 32 (48) rows without shaping.

t) Work as given for feet from *** to end.

### Ears (make two)

Make one the reverse of the other.

u) Cast on 2 sts and work 1 row.

v) Inc one st at the same edge of every row until there are 8 sts.

*Do I hear a cat burglar?*
TABBY

w) Dec one st at the same edge as before on every alt row until 2 sts remain.

Work 2 tog, fasten off.

**Ear linings (make two):** make one the reverse of the other.

Work as given for ears, but inc to 7 instead of 8 sts at v).

## Nose

x) Cast on 32 (48) sts and work 6 (8) rows.

y) Next row – *work 2 tog, work 4 (8), work 2 tog tbl, rep from * to end.

Next row – *work 2 tog tbl, work 2 (6), work 2 tog, rep from * to end.

Continue to decrease in this way until 8 sts rem. Run a thread through rem sts.

## To make up

To assemble the pieces, (see Fig 5), work as follows: Seam body top and base together matching shapings and fill before closing up. Seam head into a sphere, insert safety eyes, fill and attach to body.

Seam tail into a tube, fill and attach flat ended, also catching the tail down to the body of the cat if preferred. Seam feet into spheres and attach to body. Note that this cat can be positioned in various ways by adjusting the head and feet. The head can also be varied so that the cat is either looking up or at an angle. Stitch ear linings flat inside ears and attach ears to head.

Add details – see finishing instructions on page 6.

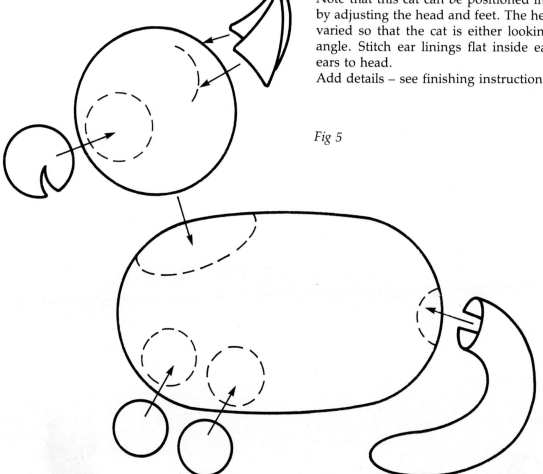

*Fig 5*

*I feel like sleeping for 1001 nights*
WHITE PERSIAN

*Just taking a cat nap*
TORTOISESHELL AND WHITE CAT

## Tabby.

I gave this little tabby embroidered 'eye make-up' and strong white whiskers, (see page 9). She is approximately 38 cm (15 in) long.

### Materials

Random-dyed DK, 3 × 50 gm balls in brown and black mix.
DK scraps for embroidery.
Approximately 250 gm (9 oz) washable filling.
1 pair medium sized safety cat's eyes.

### Tension

22 sts and 28 rows = 10 cm (4 in) in st st on 4 mm needles. 4 mm needles are used throughout.

### Pattern

Work as for basic pattern for curled up cat in st st throughout, making only 2 feet instead of 4.

**Special notes**: The pieces are brushed on the st st side before making up. I curled the cat's tail around her and attached it by the end, so that she only needs front feet as the back feet do not show.

## Tortoiseshell and white

I used three colours to give a patchwork effect, (see opposite page). This cat is approximately 43 cm (17 in) long.

### Materials

Mohair, 1 × 50 gm ball each of white, black and ginger.
DK scraps for embroidery.
Approximately 250 gm (9 oz) washable filling.
1 pair large sized safety cat's eyes.

### Tension

18 sts and 24 rows = 10 cm (4 in) in st st on 4½ mm needles. 4½ mm needles are used throughout.

### Pattern

Make the basic pattern for the curled up cat in the larger size in st st in the following colours:
Work the head in black.
Work 4 feet in any of the 3 colours.
Tail – cast on in black, work 15 rows in black at s), then 18 rows ginger, complete in white.
Ears – one white, one black.
Ear linings – one ginger, one white.
Nose – cast on and work 6 rows in ginger at x), complete in white.
Work the body top and base in large uneven areas patterned as you prefer in the three colours.

**Special notes**: Brush the st st side before making up and then assemble the cat in your chosen pose. I added strong white eyelines and whiskers, as well as multicoloured eyebrow whiskers, but she only needed a small dark nose.

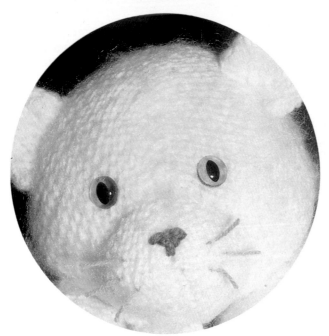

# White Persian

This cat is looking for a good home, (see page 11). Her approximate size is 43 cm (17 in) long.

## Materials

Brushed chunky 2 × 100 gm balls in white.
DK scraps for embroidery.
Approximately 250 gm (9 oz) washable filling.
1 pair large sized safety cat's eyes.

## Tension

14 sts and 18 rows = 10 cm (4 in) in st st on 6½ mm needles. 6½ mm needles are used throughout.

## Pattern

Make the basic pattern for the curled up cat in the larger size in reversed st st, but making only 2 feet.

**Special notes:** Brush all the pieces on the reversed st st side before making up, and place the front feet under the chin so that the cat is curled round in a circle. Her face simply needs a pink nose and grey whiskers.

# Playful kittens

These two little kittens are playful and mischievous, (see opposite page). Their approximate size is 30.5 cm (12 in) long.

## Materials for black and white kitten

DK, 1 × 50 gm ball each in white and black.
Scraps of DK for embroidery.
Approximately 100 gm (4 oz) washable filling.
1 pair small sized safety cat's eyes.

## Tension

24 sts and 32 rows = 10 cm (4 in) in st st on 4 mm needles. 4 mm needles are used throughout.

## Pattern

Make the basic pattern for the curled up cat in the smaller size in st st throughout in the following colours:
Make the body top and base, the head and the ears in black. Make the feet, ear linings and nose in white. For the tail, cast on and work 24 rows in black, complete in white.

## Materials for white kitten

Brushed DK, 1 × 50 gm ball in white.
Scraps of DK for embroidery.
Approximately 100 gm (4 oz) washable filling.
1 pair small safety cat's eyes.

## Tension

As for black and white kitten.

## Pattern

Make the basic pattern for the curled up cat in the smaller size in reversed st st throughout.

**Special notes:** These kittens are both illustrated in a sitting up position, ready to take on all-comers. You can also position them lying on their backs ready to play. The feet should then be stitched to the top of the body, the tail left straight, and the head facing upwards.

*A purr-fect pair*
TWO PLAYFUL KITTENS

# Lying down cats

*From the basic pattern for the lying down cat, make the grey short-haired cat, the odd-eyed white kitten, the long-haired kitten, the Siamese kitten and the rex.*

## Basic pattern

### Body

a) Cast on 7 (10) sts and work 1 row.
b) Next row – Inc one st in every st, 14 (20) sts.
Work 1 row.
c) Rep the last 2 rows twice more. 56 (80) sts.
d) Work 40 (66) rows without shaping.
e) Next row – *Work 2 tog, rep from * to end.
Work 1 row.
f) Rep the last 2 rows twice more.
Run a thread through rem 7 (10) sts.

### Head

g) Cast on 8 sts and work 1 row.
h) Next row – Inc one st in every st. (16) sts.
Work 1 row.
i) Next row – (Inc one st in next st, work 2, inc one st in next st) 4 times. (24) sts.
Work 1 row.
Next row – (Inc one st in next st, work 4, inc one st in next st) 4 times. (32) sts.
Work 1 row.
j) Cont in this way, adding 8 sts on every alt row by working 2 more sts between increasings on each increasing row, until there are 48 (72) sts.
k) Work 13 (19) rows without shaping.

l) Next row – *Work 2 tog, work 8 (14), work 2 tog tbl, rep from * to end. 40 (64) sts.
Work 1 row.
Next row – *Work 2 tog, work 6 (12), work 2 tog tbl, rep from * to end. 32 (56) sts.
Work 1 row.
m) Cont in this way, losing 8 sts on every alt row, and so working 2 sts less between decreasings on each decreasing row until there are 8 sts.
Run a thread through rem sts.

### Legs and feet (make four)

n) Cast on 20 (28) sts.
o) Work 26 (40) rows without shaping.
p) Next row – *Work 2 tog, rep from * to end.
Work 1 row. 10 (14) sts.
q) Rep the last 2 rows once more.
Run a thread through rem 5 (7) sts.

### Tail

r) Work as given for legs and feet, but work 32 (48) rows straight at o).

### Ears (make two)

Make one ear the reverse of the other.
s) Cast on 2 sts and work 1 row.
t) Inc one st at the same edge of every row until there are 8 sts.

u) Dec one st at the same edge as before on every alt row until 2 sts remain.
Work 2 tog, fasten off.

**Ear linings (make two)**: one the reverse of the other. Work as given for ears, but inc to 7 instead of 8 sts at t).

## Nose

v) Cast on 32 (48) sts and work 6 (8) rows.
w) Next row – *Work 2 tog, work 4 (8), work 2 tog tbl, rep from * to end.
Next row – *Work 2 tog tbl, work 2 (6), work 2 tog, rep from * to end.
Continue to decrease in this way until 8 sts rem.
Run a thread through rem sts.

## To make up

To assemble the pieces, (see Fig 6), work as follows: Seam body piece into a tube and fill before closing up, placing this and all other seams downwards. Seam legs and tail into a tube, leaving cast on edge open. Fill and attach legs flat ended beneath body. Fill and attach tail open ended.

Seam head into a sphere, insert safety eyes, fill and attach to the body. Note that the position of the head can be varied to that the cat is looking up, forward or at an angle. Seam side edges of nose, fill and attach to head by the cast on edge.

Stitch ear linings flat inside ears and attach ears to head.

Add detail – see finishing instructions on page 6.

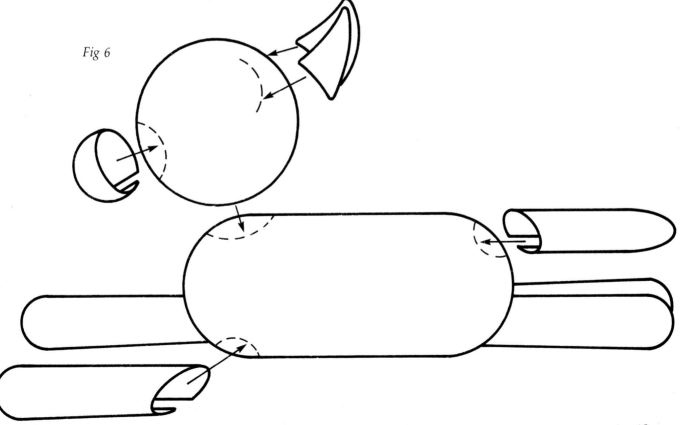

*Fig 6*

# The grey short-hair.

This cat is lanky but otherwise very plain and his approximate size is 38 cm (15 in) long (see opposite).

## Materials

Brushed DK, 2 × 50 gm balls in dark grey.
DK scraps for embroidery.
About 150 gm (5 oz) of washable filling.
1 pair medium safety cats' eyes and 1 medium safety nose.

## Tension

24 sts and 32 rows = 10 cm (4 in) in st st on 4 mm needles. 4 mm needles are used throughout.

## Pattern

Make the basic pattern for the lying down cat in the smaller size, but add 12 extra rows to the body at d), the legs at o), and the tail at r), working in st st throughout.

**Special notes**: I gave this cat a safety nose which shows up well on his dark colour, and then stitched white whiskers in to his ears for added character.

# Long haired kitten

This little kitten needs to be brushed every day, (see opposite). She is approximately 30.5 cm (12 in) long.

## Materials

Brushed DK, 2 × 40 gm balls in grey.
DK scraps for embroidery.
Approximately 100 gm (4 oz) washable filling.
1 pair medium safety cat's eyes.

## Tension

22 sts and 28 rows = 10 cm (4 in) in st st on 4 mm needles. 4mm needles are used throughout.

## Pattern

Make the smaller size of the basic pattern for the lying down cat, in reversed st st throughout.

**Special notes**: The reversed st st pieces are brushed, and I added fairly strong features that show up on the grey, including a dark area above the nose, and pale 'eyebrows'.

# Siamese kitten

This kitten's 'eye make-up' gives her the oriental look, (see opposite). Her size is approximately 28 cm (11 in) long.

## Materials

DK, 1 × 50 gm ball in beige, and a small quantity of chocolate brown.
DK scraps for embroidery.
Approximately 100 gm (4 oz) washable filling.
1 pair small blue safety cat's eyes.

## Tension

24 sts and 32 rows = 10 cm (4 in) in st st on 4 mm needles. 4 mm needles are used throughout.

## Pattern

Make the basic pattern for the lying down cat in the smaller size in st st in the following colours:
Body, head and ear linings in beige, nose and ears in brown.
Legs and feet – cast on and work the first 20 rows at o) in beige, complete in brown.
Tail – cast on and work the first 20 rows in beige in the same way, complete in brown.

**Special notes**: Make up matching the colours and then add strong dark lines around the eyes and nose to give the distinctive oriental look.

*A basketful of mischief*
LONG HAIRED GREY KITTEN
GREY SHORT HAIRED CAT
AND SIAMESE KITTEN

*Smile please*
REX AND THE ODD-EYED KITTEN

# Odd-eyed white

This pretty little odd-eyed kitten has a blue satin bow around his neck, (see opposite). He is approximately 43 cm (17 in) long.

## Materials

Brushed DK, 1 × 100 gm ball in white.
DK scraps for embroidery.
Approximately 250 gm (9 oz) washable filling.
1 pair medium safety cats eyes *in odd colours*.
Length of satin ribbon.

## Tension

24 sts and 32 rows = 10 cm (4 in) in st st on 4mm needles. 4 mm needles are used throughout.

## Pattern

Make the larger size of the basic pattern for the lying down cat, in st st throughout.

**Special notes**: The pieces for this kitten were firmly brushed before making up, and he has distinctive odd eyes. I found he needed very little embroidery, just a pink nose, brown mouth and eye markings and white whiskers.

# Rex

The rex was knitted in 'crunchy' yarn, (see opposite), and his approximate size is 35.5 cm (14 in) long.

## Materials

DK slub, 3 × 50 gm balls in cream.
DK scraps for embroidery.
Approx 150 gm (5 oz) washable filling.
1 pair medium safety cat's eyes.

## Tension

24 sts and 32 rows = 10 cm (4 in) in st st on 4 mm needles. 4 mm needles are used throughout.

## Pattern

Work as for basic pattern for lying down cat in the smaller size, in reversed st st.

**Special notes**: Reversed st st in the crunchy yarn gives a very authentic rex feel. I added only simple, darker embroidery lines at the sides of the nose.

# Sitting cats

*From the basic pattern for the sitting cat, make the Siamese, the Persian, the ginger tom and the black and white cat.*

## Basic pattern

### Front of body

a) Cast on 36 (54) sts and work 24 (36) rows without shaping.**
b) Next row – Work 2 tog, work to end.
Next row – Work to last 2, work 2 tog.
Next row – Work 2 tog, work to end.
Next row – Work without shaping.
c) ***Rep the last 4 rows until 18 (28) sts rem.
Work 1 row.
Cast off.

### Back of body

d) Work as given for front of body as far as **.
e) Next row – Work to last 2, work 2 tog.
Next row – Work 2 tog, work to end.
Next row – Work to last 2, work 2 tog.
Next row – Work without shaping.
f) Complete as given for front of body from *** to end.

### Head

g) Cast on 8 sts and work 1 row.
h) Next row – Inc one st in every st. (16) sts.
Work 1 row.
i) Next row – (Inc one st in next st, work 2, inc one st in next st) 4 times. (24) sts.

Work 1 row.
Next row – (Inc one st in next st, work 4, inc one st in next st) 4 times. (32) sts.
Work 1 row.
j) Cont in this way, adding 8 sts on every alt row, by working 2 more sts between increasings on each increasing row, until there are 48 (72) sts.
k) Work 13 (19) rows without shaping.
l) Next row – *Work 2 tog, work 8 (14), work 2 tog tbl, rep from * to end. 40 (64) sts.
Work 1 row.
Next row – *Work 2 tog, work 6 (12), work 2 tog tbl, rep from * to end. 32 (56) sts.
Work 1 row.
m) Cont in this way, losing 8 sts on every alt row, and so working 2 sts less between decreasings on each decreasing row until there are 8 sts.
Run a thread through rem sts.

### Feet (make four)

n) Cast on 5 (7) sts and work 1 row.
o) Next row – Inc one st in every st. 10 (14) sts.
Rep the last 2 rows once more. 20 (28) sts.
p) Work 6 (8) rows without shaping.
q) ***Next row – *Work 2 tog, rep from * to end. 10 (14) sts.

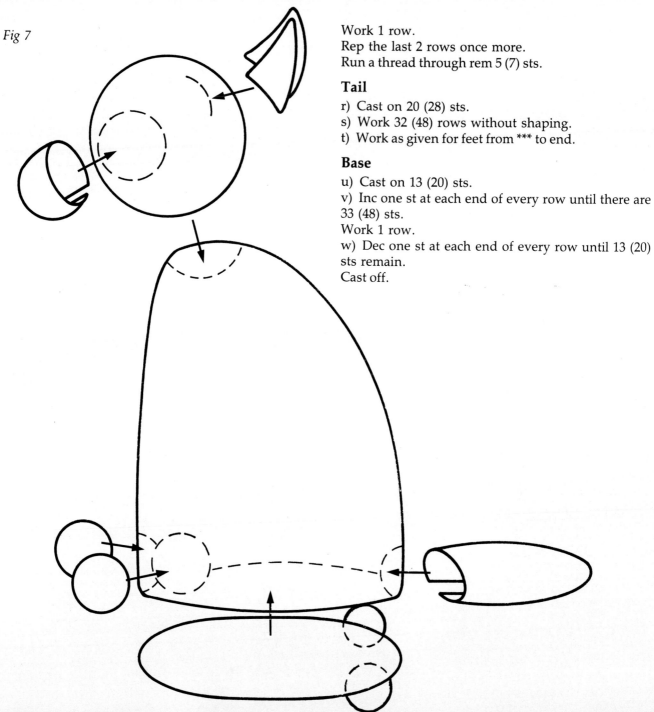

*Fig 7*

Work 1 row.
Rep the last 2 rows once more.
Run a thread through rem 5 (7) sts.

### Tail

r) Cast on 20 (28) sts.
s) Work 32 (48) rows without shaping.
t) Work as given for feet from *** to end.

### Base

u) Cast on 13 (20) sts.
v) Inc one st at each end of every row until there are 33 (48) sts.
Work 1 row.
w) Dec one st at each end of every row until 13 (20) sts remain.
Cast off.

## Ears (make two)

Make one the reverse of the other.

x) Cast on 2 sts and work 1 row.

y) Inc one st at the same edge of every row until there are 8 sts.

z) Dec one st at the same edge as before on every alt row until 2 sts remain.

Work 2 tog, fasten off.

**Ear linings (make two)**: make one the reverse of the other.

Work as for ears, but inc to 7 instead of 8 sts at y).

## Nose

aa) Cast on 32 (48) sts and work 6 (8) rows.

bb) Next row – *work 2 tog, work 4 (8), work 2 tog tbl, rep from * to end.

Next row – *work 2 tog tbl, work 2 (6), work 2 tog, rep from * to end.

Continue to decrease in this way until 8 sts rem.

Run a thread through rem sts.

## To make up

To assemble the pieces, (see Fig 7), work as follows:
Seam body halves together, matching shaping, insert base and fill before closing up.

Seam head into a sphere, insert safety eyes, fill and attach, noting that the angle of the head can be varied as you wish.

Seam feet into spheres, fill and attach to body. Seam tail into a tube, fill and attach to body open ended. Stitch ear linings flat inside ears and attach ears to head.

Add details – see finishing instructions on page 6.

# Blue Persian

This kitten needs to be brushed vigorously to give the Persian look, (see page 25). He is approximately 25.5 cm (10 in) high.

## Materials

Brushed chunky, 2 × 100 gm balls in grey.
DK scraps for embroidery.
Approximately 400 gm (14 oz) washable filling.
1 pair large safety cat's eyes.

## Tension

14 sts and 18 rows = 10 cm (4 in) in st st on 6½ mm needles. 6½ mm needles are used throughout.

## Pattern

Make the smaller size from the basic pattern for the sitting cat in st st with the following variations:
Work 30 rows without shaping on the body pieces at a).

Work 23 rows without shaping on the head at k).

Work 6 rows without shaping on the nose at aa).

**Special note**: I added frown lines between the eyes and an unsmiling mouth to give the Persian expression. The nose is pink, and there are matching white whiskers in the ears.

# Black and white

This cuddly cat needs very little detail added, (see page 29). His approximate size is 28 cm (11 in) high.

## Materials

Brushed DK, 1 × 100 gm balls each of black and white.
DK scraps for embroidery.
Approximately 200 gm (7 oz) washable filling.
1 pair medium safety cat's eyes.

## Tension

24 sts and 32 rows = 10 cm (4 in) in st st on 4 mm needles. 4 mm needles are used throughout.

## Pattern

Make the smaller size from the basic pattern for the sitting cat in st st in the following colours:
Work ear linings, nose and feet in white.
Work base and ears in black.
Cast on and work the first 16 rows of the tail in black, complete in white.
Front of body – work the first row at a): 26 sts black, 10 sts white. Keep these sts in these colours throughout the rem of the work, so working a white strip up the unshaped edge.
Back of body, as for front of body, *but* work the first row 10 sts white, 26 sts black, so making this piece the reverse of the front.

**Special note**: brush all the pieces and match colours where applicable. This cat's markings make him so striking that he needed no more detail than a pink nose and white whiskers.

# Ginger tom

This cat has tiger-like markings and long whiskers, (see opposite). He is approximately 23 cm (9 in) high.

## Materials

Random-dyed DK, 1 × 50 gm ball in ginger-orange mix.
DK scraps for embroidery.
Approximately 200 gm (7 oz) washable filling.
1 pair medium sized safety cat's eyes.

## Tension

22 sts and 28 rows = 10 cm (4 in) in st st on 4 mm needles. 4 mm needles are used throughout.

## Pattern

Make the smaller size from the basic pattern for the sitting cat in st st.

**Special note**: To give the tigerish expression I added strong stripes outside the eyes, white lines below the eyes and brown eyebrows. The mouth and nose are a strong, dark brown, and the whiskers are long.

# Siamese

The Siamese's eyes are embroidered in blue and she is wearing a new red collar, (see opposite). She is approximately 33 cm (13 in) high.

## Materials

DK, 1 × 50 gm ball in beige, plus a small quantity of chocolate brown.
DK scraps for embroidery.
Approximately 200 gm (7 oz) washable filling.
Collar.

## Tension

24 sts and 32 rows = 10 cm (4 in) in st st on 4 mm needles. 4 mm needles are used throughout.

## Pattern

Make the larger size of the basic pattern for the sitting cat in the following colours and variations:
Work the body in beige, casting on only 46 sts for the front and back at a), and decreasing down to 20 sts at c).
Work the head and ear linings in beige.
Work the nose, ears and feet in brown.
Work the first 40 rows of the tail at s) in beige, complete in brown.

**Special notes**: I embroidered the distinctive oriental eyes in blue rather than using the toy safety eyes, and I added eyelines in brown and a strong nose marking in beige. The nose is pale, and the whiskers are as long as possible.

*Cats' chorus*
BLACK AND WHITE CAT, SIAMESE AND GINGER TOM

# Helping hand

If you are a complete beginner at knitting, or your skills are a little rusty, the following information will be helpful.

Place the needle holding the stitches in the left hand and hold the working needle and the yarn in the right hand. Control the yarn by winding it round the fingers of the right hand, (see Fig 8).

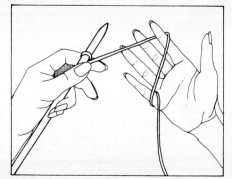

Fig 8 controlling the yarn tension

## Casting on

Begin with a slip loop about 15 cm (6 in) from the end of the yarn and tighten it on to the left-hand needle (see Fig 9). Insert the right-hand needle into the front of the loop, left to right, wind the yarn round the right-hand needle point and draw it through to the front (see Figs 10 and 11). Transfer the loop from the right-hand needle to the left-hand needle. Continue in this way, but insert the needle *between* the stitches on the left-hand needle, (see Fig 12), until you have the correct number of stitches.

## To knit stitches

Hold the yarn at the back of the work. Insert the right-hand needle into the first stitch on the left-hand needle from front to back, left to right (see Fig 13). This is known as 'knitwise'. Pass the yarn round the right-hand needle point, (see Fig 14) and draw the loop through to the front of the work, (see Fig 15). Slip the stitch off the left-hand needle (see Fig 16). Continue in this way along the row until you have transferred all the stitches to the right-hand needle. Turn the work and hold it in the left hand in preparation for the next row.

## To purl stitches

With the yarn at the front of the work, insert the right-hand needle into the front of the first stitch on the left-hand needle from right to left (see Fig 17). This is known as 'purlwise'. Pass the yarn round the right-hand needle point (see Fig 18). Draw the loop through (see Fig 19), then slip the stitch off the left-hand needle (see Fig 20). Continue in this way along the row.

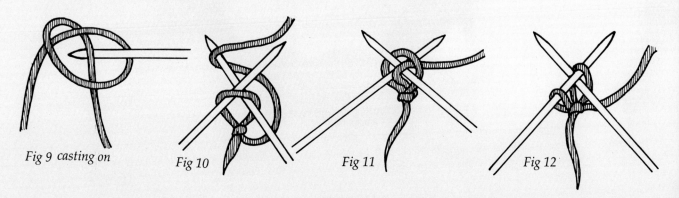

Fig 9 casting on          Fig 10          Fig 11          Fig 12

# Knit stitch

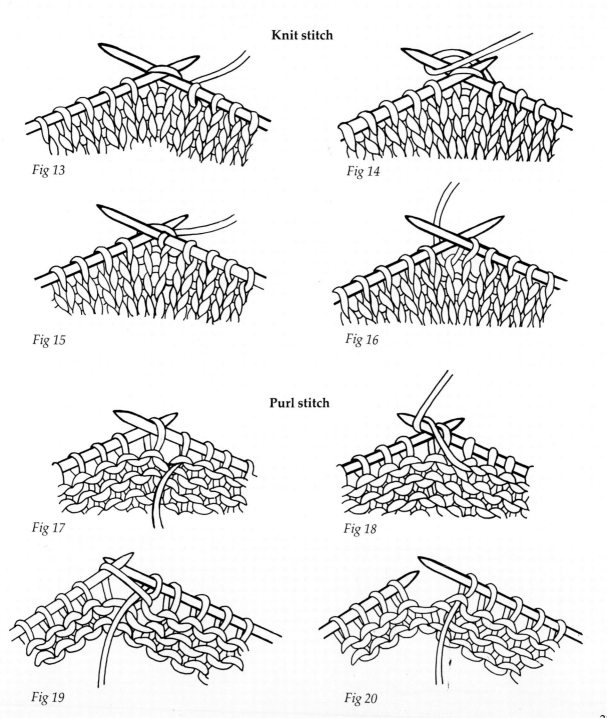

Fig 13

Fig 14

Fig 15

Fig 16

# Purl stitch

Fig 17

Fig 18

Fig 19

Fig 20

First published in Great Britain 1987
Search Press Ltd
Wellwood, North Farm Road,
Tunbridge Wells, Kent TN2 3DR

Reprinted 1989, 1990, 1995

Photographs by Search Press Studios

The author would like to thank Anne Wilcox for all her help

ISBN 0 85532 602 6

Typeset by Scribe Design, Gillingham, Kent
Made and printed in Spain by
Artes Graphicas Elkar, S. Coop.
Autonomía, 71 - 48012-Bilbao - Spain.

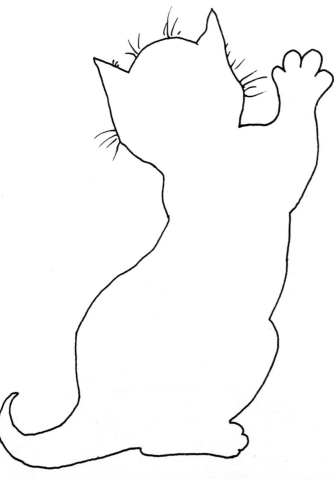